Leila Aboulela.
Photograph by Maggie Miller, © 1999.

Wish I Was Here

a Scottish multicultural anthology

Wish I Was Here

Edited by
Kevin MacNeil and Alec Finlay

pocketbooks
Morning Star Publications
Polygon
The Travelling Gallery
National Galleries of Scotland

2000

Published by:
pocketbooks
Canongate Venture (5), New Street, Edinburgh, EH8 8BH.

Morning Star Publications
Canongate Venture (5), New Street, Edinburgh, EH8 8BH.

Polygon
22 George Square, Edinburgh, EH8 9LF.

The Travelling Gallery
City Art Centre, 2 Market Street, Edinburgh, EH1 1DE.

National Galleries of Scotland
Belford Road, Edinburgh, EH4 3DS.

Typeset in Minion and Univers.
Typesetting and artworking by Bluelines Media Services.
Design concept by Lucy Richards with Alec Finlay.
Printed and bound by Redwood Books Limited, Trowbridge.
Printed on Munken Elk 90gsm available from Trebruk UK Limited.

Published with the assistance of grants from the Scottish Arts Council National
Lottery Fund, the Highlands and Islands Enterprise (HI Arts), and Comhairle Nan
Leabhraichean (The Gaelic Books Council). Chuidich Comhairle nan Leabhraichean
am foillsichear le cosgaisean an leabhair seo.

A CIP record is available from the British Library.

ISBN 0 7486 62812

List of Contents

9   List of Photographs

11   Editors' Acknowledgements

15   Introduction
Kevin MacNeil

25   Aliens' Gate

53   Speaking in Tongues

89   Voyager

117 Scent of Memory

143 Bhangra!

175 And My Fate Was Scotland
Leila Aboulela

193 Author/Photographer Notes

201 Index of Authors

203 Acknowledgements

     Aeolus CD 'Wish I Was Here'

List of Photographs

43-51	Iseult Timmermans
79-87	Craig Mackay
107-115	Elsie Mitchell
133-141	David Williams
165-173	Catriona Grant
183-191	Chila Kumari Burman

Editors' Acknowledgements

We would like to thank all of the poets for their contributions and their willingness to share their personal experiences. *Wish I Was Here* had its origins in the meetings of Asian-Scots and Gaelic poets at Speaking in Tongues, a project which brought writers from various cultural backgrounds together, run by Janet Paisley in Glasgow in 1997. Our thanks go to Janet and all of the participants.

We would also like to thank the photographers whose portraits of the poets are reproduced here. Their work is the result of commissions initiated by the Travelling Gallery and realised with the support of the Scottish Arts Council National Lottery Fund. The photographers were chosen by a panel including Alison Chisholm (Travelling Gallery), Julie Lawson and Sara Stevenson (Scottish National Portrait Gallery), Jane Warrilow (City Art Centre, Edinburgh), Catriona MacInnes and Robin Gillanders. We would like to take this opportunity to thank the selectors. In particular, we would like to acknowledge the crucial contribution of Catriona MacInnes, who interviewed many of the poets and devised the educational aspect of the project.

In addition we would like to thank the following individuals and organisations: Lisa Kapur at the Scottish Arts Council; James Holloway and Duncan Forbes at the Scottish National Portrait Gallery; Janis Adams and Lindsay Isaacs at the National Galleries of Scotland; Catherine McInerney, Literature Development Officer for Glasgow City Council; the Scottish Poetry Library; Zoë Irvine and Aeolus; the Gaelic Books Council (Comhairle Nan Leabhraichean) and particularly Ian MacDonald for his helpful comments on the manuscript; Ronald Black; Cluny Sheeler and Simon Williams at Bluelines; Alison Humphry and Ken Cockburn at pocketbooks; Alison Bowden at Polygon; Thomas Evans; and Lucy Richards, for her design concept.

The *Wish I Was Here* exhibition is at the Scottish National Portrait Gallery from 14 September 2000 until 14 January 2001, and thereafter tours Scotland with the Travelling Gallery.

Alec Finlay & Kevin MacNeil

Many thanks to family and friends (to mention all of you would take a book in itself!); everyone involved with the Iain Crichton Smith Writing Fellowship; everyone involved with Cuairt nam Bàrd 2000 (especially Adelaide Nic Charthaigh, Freda Nic Ghiolla Chathain, John Storey, Cathal O' Searcaigh, Dòmhnall MacPhilip, Màiri Nic a' Ghobhainn, Mòrag NicLeòid agus Ailean MacEanraig) and – the Blue Men (still surfacing).

Kevin MacNeil

Introduction

This is a book about identity, only more so. 'The greatest thing in the world,' wrote Michel de Montaigne, 'is to know how to be oneself.' Each of the writers in this book has their own special reasons for exploring aspects of identity (personal, cultural, ethnic, national, etc) and each of them does so in their own uniquely tantalising fashion, all the while manipulating their language(s) in appropriately diverse ways. Place, longing, belonging, exile, worldview, tolerance, tension, tradition, innovation and language itself are just some of the issues deftly – sometimes shockingly – examined in this surprisingly peerless anthology. I could think of no reason, when I first conceived of *Wish I Was Here*, as to why no editor(s) had been *Here* before and I am still mystified.

This is not, however, a timidly apologetic, overly politically-correct collection that will obligingly beg for or effortlessly expect space in the literary reviews and the clever bookshelves. It is, first and foremost, an anthology of some of the most captivating literature being created in and about Scotland at the moment. Scotland is more multicultural today than ever; this book is not as diverse as her. Various groups or individuals who were invited to submit work neglected to do so; and in any case the overall governing criterion for inclusion of relevant work was not perfunctory one hundred per cent multicultural representation but, above all, sheer writing quality. Having said that, this anthology certainly does harbour a good number of voices and ideas. It does not always make for comfortable reading and, while diversity no doubt engenders its own composite unity (one moon, many reflections), this very diversity necessitates that not every reader will agree with – or even like – every poem by every poet in this collection equally.

That, perhaps, is human nature.

A few years ago a project – variously co-ordinated by Eona Craig, Patricia Grant, Catherine McInerney and Janet Paisley – was set up in

Glasgow to bring writers from various backgrounds together for poetry performance. The project was entitled 'Speaking in Tongues' and initially involved Mohammed Kiani, Selina Mirza, Suhayl Saadi and Gerry Singh. Myself, too, but I was then working at the BBC and missed all but the final rehearsal. No matter. Under Janet Paisley's expert direction the rehearsal was seamless, confidence-instilling and – intriguing. I had never met any of these writers before and I was struck by the originality and the importance of their work. Why were these writers not widely published?

Our first poetry performance as a collective was part of an Asian Youth Festival in Glasgow's Tramway Theatre. It was a success – so much so that it seemed a shame not to carry on the 'Speaking in Tongues' collaboration. Hamid Shami came on board, as did the phenomenal percussionist Vijay Kangutkar. We did readings and workshops at various schools, libraries and radio stations around Glasgow. Friendships blossomed, literary resolve strengthened. Lasting memories took root: Vijay's hands making a hypnotic instrument of all they touched (during one rehearsal, for example, the floor of Suhayl's flat); the profound, lilting cadences of Mohammed Kiani's songpoems, not unlike Gàidhlig psalms; the quietly shimmering words of Selina Mirza, then only 16; the easy charm of Gerry Singh's poetry coming alive on the stage; Suhayl Saadi's classic short story 'Bandanna', which I nagged him to publish over slow cappuccinos in the Cul-de-Sac's Attic; Hamid Shami's unforgettable readings, at once soft and bullet-sharp, of those brief and lasting poems.

There were many aspects of the 'Speaking in Tongues' collaboration that appealed to me. As a Gàidhlig-speaker (and therefore a member of an eroded minority), as a Gàidheal exiled in an alien city, as a Gàidheal whose education was biased towards non-Gàidhlig cultures (classical literature and history, English history), as a Gàidheal and therefore the survivor of an inherited system of persecution, as a Gàidheal and therefore one who was brought up on the 'periphery', far from a remote and ignorant government, as a person who felt the need to externalise the contingencies and contradictions of living in a place in which I did and did not feel a sense of belonging, as a person with the need to sew up all these deepening wounds with a pen – I felt I had much in common with my Asian-Scots colleagues.

There is no Scotland, I began more fully to comprehend.

There are Scotlands.

* * *

It is eminently appropriate that circumstances have so melded that I am writing this introduction while on a tour of Ireland with other poets and musicians, a tour that is at once a (distant) homecoming and a (familiar) homeleaving. On Sunday afternoon I sat, the sweating seat stuck to my jeans, 16,000 feet up, watching the plane's cannon-like shadow arrowing smoothly over the yellowgreen limegreen browngreen fields, the villages, the towns, the lochs, the coastal beach like the naked line after a sunburnt haircut, the mind-deep sea, the clouds disintegrating and ghosting past – and all the while the plane was high and trembling as if with excitement.

It was about halfway through the flight that I realised that the seat in front of me – indeed every seat on the plane – was covered with designer-illegible handwriting, half-random lines of English and Irish. My amusement on noticing this legitimate scribbling, this sanctioned graffiti, turned to wonder. I thought about how it related to the book – this book you have in your hands – that was then sealed in the laptop in the compartment above my head. Yes: the half-hidden made public, unexpected words journeying to new places … but. This book is not about obscurity, superficiality, tokenism.

I picked up an in-flight magazine and studied the advertisements. A glossy page for Butler's Irish Handmade Chocolate sang the praises: 'History repeating itself. Thank goodness.' The recipe for the chocolate, you see, was invented in 1932 '… at a time when we Irish were more given to frugality than frivolity.' In the same magazine was an advert featuring a light description (derived from traditional Irish mythology) of the battle between Fionn MacCumhnaill and Diarmuid for the love of Grainne during which the combatants' shields were turned to mirrors. 'These polished pewter cufflinks represent the shields of the two warriors. £14 or I£17-78.'

How much more imaginative, authentic and lasting were the images actively crowding for space in the mirrored screen of my laptop's *Wish*. Despite the many similarities between the linguistic techniques of advertising and those of poetry, it seems to me that only one of these constitutes an essential art. The individual voices in this anthology subvert, disrupt, puncture and sometimes annihilate easy stereotypes. I spent the rest of the flight re-absorbing the magnificent poetry in this collection and when we touched down in Dublin and readied ourselves for a drive to Belfast my only regret was that I hadn't taken my own illegible pen to the seats and added a quotation or two from this book. For art's sake.

* * *

The trip around Ireland ignites slow-burning images in my mind. At a reading in a venue called Ionad Ghlor na nGael (the Place of the Glory of the Gàidheal) situated on the Falls Road in Belfast, among burning tablefuls of tinily ferocious candles, the poet Gearoid Mac Lochlainn, along with his mandolin player and Jamaican saxophone player, is singing a jazz-tinged reggae song. In Irish. It touches me in ways the most plaintive Gàidhlig lament could. By the walls of Derry a hardcore dance tune is slamming forth from a distant music shop and a friend from the South picks up on the beat, idly practises her Irish dance steps, naturally, unselfconsciously. At Bunscoil Cholm Cille (an Irish language primary school in Derry) after talks and music and readings from our party, the pupils sing us a Beatles song. In Irish. Recognising internationally-renowned Irish poet Cathal O' Searcaigh's house in Donegal before we've seen it is easy due to the tell-tale parallel-line explosions of technicolour prayer flags, like fluorescent *drais* on a dozen Highland washing lines. The Donegal area and language are so similar to the Scottish that we find ourselves speaking Gàidhlig, understanding Irish.

The cultural clash of the traditional and the contemporary that is all around me chimes beautifully with the writing in this book (which tours Ireland with me as my constant companion). Literature – especially the literature of the marginalised – is taking centre-page, has never been so exciting.

Flying back, Scotland – formerly the land of the cleared, the dispossessed, the land of the sheep, currently being re-perceived as the land of the sheep, Dolly, the clone – is multiform and glittering with exquisite, melodious, hard-edged poetry, poetry that is allowing the country's three-dimensional map to sparkle in a new and penetrating light. Literary images, human correspondences, cross-cultural bridges are being constructed that shine and dazzle and overarch the old conceptions like a rainbow among the bare hills of clouds.

* * *

Just as no language is taboo, just as no use of language is taboo, so, too, there is no subject matter that is not open to the poet's free scrutiny. This anthology energetically leaps around the spectrum of human experience like a frog eating lightning. Writers of international renown, up-and-coming writers and fresh-on-the-scene writers share and dispute ideas on everything from homesickness to sport to electrical Punjabis. From the perfect, devastating lyricism of Jackie Kay to the uncompromising and sensuous imagination of aonghas macneacail, from the richer-than-gold prose-poetry of Leila Aboulela to the spare, muscular dynamism of Hamid Shami's high-performance poetry, this collection, I'm sure, offers enduring treats for all people interested in poetry, in culture … in people.

Returning 'home' from Ireland, black-clad, unshaven, exhausted after the week's readings, visits, interviews, I am greeted by an officer at the airport security desk with half-concealed suspicion. His eyes meet mine. "I.D." he growls. "Passport."

I hunch wearily over my rucksack, thrust my hand in and feel around the jumble of clothes and books for my passport. My hand spiders across a well-thumbed document: the MS for *Wish I Was Here.*

And during the appropriately long time it takes to find that elusive passport, this darkly stooped figure, hunched in his boots, resembles, for all the world, nothing more than – what – a question mark?

Kevin MacNeil / Caoimhin MacNeill

Kensaleyre
Portree
Glasgow
Belfast
Derry
Gortahork
Dublin
Kensaleyre

April-May 2000

Ceann Sail Eighre
Port Rìgh
Glaschu
Beal Feirste
Doire Chaluim Chille
Gort a' Choirce
Baile Atha Cliath
Ceann Sail Eighre

An Giblean-An Ceitean 2000

Lost

To quote my distant friend Imran MacLeod,
'A man with no culture has no identity.'

The last I heard from him was, he was off
To the Himalayas.

He had a very confused childhood.

Father was Scottish,
Mother Pakistani.

They'd always be arguing over many things
Concerning him.

One was religion.

Father wanted him brought up
A Catholic; mother wanted a Muslim.

Was the only boy on our street who went
To mosque on Fridays and chapel on Sundays.

But in the mountains

God's sure to find him.

Hamid Shami

Aliens' Gate

When I First Came to Scotland …

I pushed open the door that said 'Black Bastards' in pen, and stepped into the mosque. A woman was taking off her shoes, untying laces, left shoe then right. I greeted her and after she replied, I said, "Where can I get soap and water to clean the words off the door?"

She said, "Leave it now, we must be quick."

I took off my shoes and hurried after her down corridors thick with toddlers, little girls in long braids, fights over bubble-gum.

When I reached the hall, I heard a loud voice, "Straighten the lines! Straighten the lines and pray as if this is the last prayer."

Leila Aboulela

At the Aliens' Gate

I
The one saying

> You have no street
> You have no town
> Your voice is nothing we know

is the one who pushed the burning rag
through the letterbox

The one saying

> You have no voice
> Your voice is nothing

is the uniformed man at the Aliens' Gate
willing himself to believe
that the person
with the careful suitcase
is out to put one over on him
has uprooted himself from his own language
in order to do this

The man at the Aliens' Gate
carrying in his suitcase the floods of the rainy season
is darker than he is   braver

II

Scotland   my touchpaper
red rag to an enraged girl

I become a stranger again
listener   to foreign tongues
strange utterances
from those who consider their speech
to be commonplace and true
repeated, made perfect   each consonant
a wheel turning a whole revolution
in the mouth

      You have no street
      You have no town
      You have no voice

My voice no longer fits me

Another woman
is a wee wifey asking me to tea
      There is a gale above Glen Shiel
      I am broken in two
      Help me to be made whole

But I become a stranger
close up   a bog asphodel
whispering
      I will not   be broken

Gerrie Fellows

Asylum Seeker

It is a demonstration
that the system works
said the prison service

when Enahoro Esemuze
wrapped a strip of blanket
around his throat

and hanged his
scarredNigerian body
in his detention cell.

He was spotted
before he harmed himself
seriously

said the prison service.

Irfan Merchant

My Talented Cousin

Out each morning,
delivering
papers.

Afternoons spent
behind a shop
counter.

Evenings
Indian restaurant –
very exclusive,
waitering.

Never stops.

He's got
two degrees,
business and philosophy.

Hamid Shami

An Gàidheal
The Pakistani

'underneath the pavement there is the beach' – may 68

1

anns gach baile brònach
in every mournful city
fon phavement fhiadhaich
underneath pavements growing wild
tha tràigh gad ionndrain
there is a beach that longs for you
bata na do làmh
a walking stick in your hand
bàta na do shùilean
a boat in your eyes

2

neapaicin geal
a white handkerchief
mar isean air an iteig
like a bird on the wing
an-dè aig a' phort-adhair
yesterday at the airport
an-diugh na do phòcaid
today in your pocket

tha an saoghal a' fàs nas lugha
the world is growing smaller
's an taigh nas motha
and the house bigger
tha a' chlann a' fàs mòr
the children are growing up
gad fhàgail le fotos is telebhisean
leaving you with photographs and television

ceann air balla neo air bocsa
a head on a wall or on a box
ann an leabhar neo ann an sgàthan
in a book or in a mirror

cumaidh tu ort, le na soithichean 's le na sgòthan
you will keep on with the dishes and the clouds
an sian nad chùlaibh
the rain at your back
seòladair nan speuran
sailor of the skies

3

eadar breith is bàs tha B&B ann an Glaschu

between the births and deaths there is a B&B in Glasgow

eadar prìs chaorach is prìs cruidh tha caitheamh-beatha

between the price of sheep and that of cattle there is a livelihood

eadar clach is cladh tha cuimhne

between a stone and a grave there is a memory

4.

tha goirt san tìr

famine is in the land

is pian nad amhaich

and a pain is in your throat

tha blas cànain

the taste of a language

fhathast air do theanga

lingers on the tongue

's an t-acras ort

and you are hungry

5
le leac-uaghach an àite cluasaig
with a tombstone for a pillow
chan fhaigh thu mòran cadail
you won't get much sleep

6
air do ghlùinean ann an cidsin
on your knees in a kitchen
neo ann an achadh
or in a field
ach seasaidh do chreideamh
with your faith still standing.

India Gate

The noon sun over Delhi
Lit up the M8.

On my soft shoulder
Was a hard shoulder
Laying out a long carpet
To the pink city of Jaipur.

Looking towards the Lomonds
I saw a lama
On the cooling heights of Shimla
Walking on a cloud of dust.

And a small train
Rattling the iron gauges
Fuelling a trip to the Ganges.

Waiting on the platform
At Varanasi
I met so many strangers
Who had been here before.

Watched them
Bathing in the warm light
Where Emperors had stood
Not hearing the thundering clatter
Of the Raj.

And reflected in the churned
Up waters of the flood
Was a lovely child of both.

Gerry Singh

An Gàidheal Glas

Is mise 'n Gàidheal Glas.

Rugadh mi am broinn
Màthair na Talmhainn.

Chuir Mnathan nan Cat-Fraoich
Mar dhleasdanas orm 's mar fhiachaibh
A' Bhratach-Shìth' a chumail
An àird air feadh an t-saoghail.

Chan eil san t-saoghal seo ach dubhar.
Chan eil san t-saoghal cheart ach bruadar.

Chan fhaigh m' aigne suaimhneas
Gus an tèid mo leigeil am bàs,
Sùghta do thalamh mo dhùthchais.

Rody Gorman

Gael

Me Gael.

Me born in belli
Land Moder.

Wile Kat Wimmin they say
Hey yu
Keep up Flag of Peace, see,
Whole world see.

World – shadow!
Real world – dream!

Not rest
Till they lower me down
Sucked back earth.

Rody Gorman

An Duine Dubh
The Highlander

dachaigh air do dhruim
  a home on your back
bùth air do bhaidhsagail
  a shop on your bicycle
dh'fhosgladh tu do mhàileid
  you would open your suitcase
gàire làn grèine. "Seall seo!"
  with a smile as wide as sunshine. "Look at this!"

lingerie an lingerbay
  lingerie in lingerbay
sìoda ann an làmhan cruaidh a' chroiteir
  silk in the rough hands of a crofter
sìol ùr bho fad' às
  new seed from far away
cho aotrom, cho àlainn
  so light, so beautiful

a' siubhal am measg shrainnsearan
  travelling among strangers
cothromaichte le feansaichean is cinn-theagaisg
  weighted down by fenceposts and texts
cha robh nad cheum
  only memory and homesickness
ach cuimhne is cianalas
  to dog your step

a' bàsachadh leis an fhuachd
catching your death of cold
reic thu d' aodach
you sold your clothes
's thog thu teine, taigh is teaghlach
and you built a fire, a house and raised a family
an-diugh tha do bhùithtean làn dhaoine
today your shops are full of people
's do mhàileid a' feitheamh
and your suitcase is waiting
tha na làithean-saora a' fàs nas daoire
the holidays are getting dearer
a-nis nach eil ach deilbh rin togail
now there are only photographs to take

babs nicgriogair

Rose Street to Mecca

We go to the Indian restaurant in Rose Street. My birthday and yours. We were born in the same month, we look alike. In our wedding, my aunt said that Adam and Eve looked alike and I was dizzy, I couldn't eat.

Fourteen years later you order Fish Pakora, Nan Keema, Karahi King Prawns. I eat my Lamb Nentara and the taste goes through my blood, surreal. "Forever," I say to you, "I will want this dish and nothing else."

The waiter comes to our table. Radiant, as if he has known us for years. You talk with him as he opens out his restaurant napkin. He tells us he's going on *hajj*, the pilgrimage to Mecca, and his eyes shine even more. "That's it," he says, lifting our empty plates up high, "this time next week I'll be, *insha' Allah*, in the lighted-up city."

Iseult Timmermans

Gerry Singh

babs nicgriogair

Rob MacKenzie

Speaking in Tongues

Sam But Different

Ha'in, fae da start, mair is ee wye o spaekin
o makkin sense o things, we learn ta fit
whit we say ta whit's lippened. Takk pity apö dem
at's born ta wan tongue: dem at nivver preeve
maet fae idder tables. Raised wi twa languages
is unconscious faestin: twa wyes o tinkin.
Een extends da tidder; can shaa wis anidder wirld
yet foo aa wirlds ir jöst da sam, but different.

Sam – same
da – the
mair is – more than
lippened – expected
apö – on
demat's – those who are
preeve – taste a morsel
maet – food
idder – other

Christine De Luca

Cànain

Bha am beòil mar ghlagan fhlùraichean,
tais, domhainn, fàilteachail,
is bha an cainnt na cùbhraidheachd
a dh'fhalbh air a' ghaoith
nuair a bha an samhradh aca seachad
is a shearg iad dhan ùir.

Bidh beòil eile a' nochdadh ann,
cuimir, gleansach, guanach,
am bilean den aon chorcarachd
ris an fheadhainn a dh'aom,
is seach gu bheil maitheas san talamh
carson a bhiodh am boltrach staoin?

Meg Bateman

Language

Their mouths were like the bells of flowers,
moist, deep, welcoming,
and their talk was a fragrance
which disappeared on the breeze
when their summer was over
and they crumpled into dust.

Other mouths will come,
shapely, shining, winsome,
their lips of the same crimson
as the ones that are gone,
and as there is a goodness in the soil
why need I doubt that they will be as sweet?

Meg Bateman

Famously Ethnic

As a spokesman
For my people
All
I have to say
Is
Fuck
Individuality.

Hamid Shami

Just Schools

Good to know
That all our great teachers
Are
White lower middle class
Loving

Christians.

Hamid Shami

aon rud eile

tha mi air rudeigineach eile a chall
eadar a' Ghàidhlig
's a' Fhraingis
is Beurla Chanada
gam thachdadh sa choille
gam fhàgail claoidhte
an deas-meadhan butarrais teaghlaich
gam bhàthadh an siud 's an seo
a-muigh an sin sa Chaolas
Alba Nuadh air fàire
's gun de chobhair nam chòir
ach freagairt bodaich air a' fòn
"dìreach meadhanach math,
a Sheonaidh"
's cha chluinn mi an còrr

Iain S. Mac a' Phearsain

one other thing

I've lost something else
apart from Gaelic and French
and Canadian English
choking me in the woods
leaving me wasted
in the middle of a family mess
submerging me here and there
and out in the Strait
Nova Scotia horizoned
and no help in sight
but an old man's answer on the telephone
"just middling,
Johnny …"
and hearing no more

John S. MacPherson

These words're yours now
my having something to say

only translates to
a' dèanamh cromadh cinn

like a collie's shadow
there's stock on the astroturf

that the page proceeds
experience is as experience

does nothing but Narcissus
like torpor come by when

in the best social circles
as mebbe now, these words, for you

The difficult second album

a' dèanamh cromadh cinn: nodding (of the head)

Rob MacKenzie

'Se jazz a' bhaile bh'ann
snug i' the cusp 'tween

an' the old rebellion began
Union Jack thalla 's cac

Cold War chaos an' the cèilidh
Jahweh brickbat ballets

two fingers to NATO, the cùram
agus pompous American Rock

On the Castle's appropriate lawn
The sad day gone we left the croft

just three chopped chords an'
unavoidable lilt le clachan ùr'

Lewis Punk bands of the early 1980s

Rob MacKenzie

an tùr caillte

snàmh anns an eabar ghleadhrach
eadar freumhaichean
mo dhà chànan
an tè tha dearg
a' ruith na dealan brisg tro m' fhèithean
's an tèile
                  coimheach, coingeis, eòlach
mum sheice mar eideadh ciomaich 's mi
sìneadh meuran mo thuigse, mo lèirsinn
a-mach thar nan sgrìob-thonn
gus bàighean an t-saoghail a ruigheachd
gus tràighean an t-saoghail a ruigheachd
thar shligeach briste nan lid
gus cànain an t-saoghail a ruigheachd

ged nach biodh tu ach
                        thar chaolais
tha faobhar
              eadar ar briathran

seinneamaid laoidh don
chainnt a sheas binn
seinneamaid maoladh
dhan sgàinear

aonghas macneacail

the lost tower

swimming in the clangorous mud
between the roots of my two languages
the one that is red
sprinting swift lightnings through my veins
and the other
                         alien, indifferent, familiar
wrapped around my skin like prison clothes, as i
stretched out the fingers of my reason, my vision
across wavefurrows
to reach all the bays of the world
to reach all the shores of the world
across broken shellmounds of syllables
to reach the languages of the world

though you should be but
                         across a kyle
a sharp blade lies
                between our words

let us hymn the
tongue that stood sweet
let us sing blunting
to the sunderer

tùr – may be translated as either 'tower' or 'reason' or 'sanity'
bàigh – means both 'bay' and 'kindness', 'affection' or 'friendship'
sheas binn – literally 'remained melodic', but could also be interpreted as 'faced a
judgement or sentence'

aonghas macneacail

Animal Impersonations

Dog –
woof woof

Cow –
moo

Skinhead –
fuckin' – black – bastard.

Hamid Shami

Mother Tongue

Yes,
I speak
Fluent
Urdu
But
In my dreams
I bawl,
Curse
And swear
In the
Queen's
English.

Hamid Shami

Cianalas

The only word we have for *cianalas*
in the sadly inaccurate english language
is homesickness.
How can homesickness compare
to the
gut-wrenching,
mind-numbing,
soul-crunching,
foot-aching,
eye-wincing,
finely tuned melancholy
that is *cianalas*.

The weary way in which we
gauge our loss and longing.

Knowing that in the fullness
of our lives
wild horses,
CalMac winches,
faint promises
or
threats of marriage
would not drag us back
to the place of our hunger.

Siùsaidh NicNèill

Building Vocabulary

Cianalas:
Who would have thought
I'd have to come
so far from home
to find a word that perfectly captures
the voiceless ache
of having left?

A' dol dhachaigh:
Strange that I should
find restfulness
in a language where
you can never *be* home,
but only going
    homewards.

Cianalas: homesickness, longing, loneliness, melancholy
A' dol dhachaigh: going home(wards)

Christine Laennec

An Cianalas

Chuir mi 'n cianalas
Am broinn bucas
Bha 'm broinn mo chridhe
Far nach b' urrainn dha mo leòn.
Ach uairean, ar leam
Tha e faighinn a chrògan
Air iuchair na glais
'S an-dràst' 's a-rithist
Chì mi a shùilean grìogagach
A' nochadh às an dorchadas
As an tig craiteachan gainmhich
A dhòirteas beag air bheag
'S a lìonas mo chridhe
Le Tràigh Chuil
Air an coisich mi dhachaigh
Leam fhìn.

Murdo 'Stal' MacDonald

Homesickness

I have homesickness
under lock and key
boxed within my heart
where it can't harm me.
But sometimes it gets
its paws on the key
and intermittently I see
its beady eyes
peeping out in that darkness
from which a sprinkling of sand
progressively pours, filling my heart
with Coll Beach on which
I trudge home,
a cove all alone.

Murdo 'Stal' MacDonald
translated by Kevin MacNeil

Between My Two Worlds

When I left London
I wrote of English summers
Of bluebells and blackbirds
And dreamt of the snow.

I came back to Scotland
And longed for the Monsoons,
The flocks flying homewards
In the deep sunset glow.

My mother's concern, my father's care
My daughter's soft body that wasn't there;
So I switched my priorities and went back to stay
Carrying deep longings when I went away

To be enfolded in India
In its rich living spree
Yet turning to Britain
In my memory;

Till the unexpected happened
And my worlds switched again
To experience long daylight
And pine for the rain

Of a country burning
With the sun and my pain
Of living between two worlds
That I cannot maintain.

While my mother falters
And my father grows old
I hold this   my country
As my daughter holds.

Bashabi Fraser

3.3.2000

Ann am Mosambique
tuiltean uabhasach. Rugadh
leanabh ann an craoibh.

Chan eil fhios againn
gu bheil sinn beò. Chan eil sinn
beò, 's dòcha, tioram.

Bho seo a-mach bidh
na craobhan a' sgiamhail rium
nuair bhios e sileadh.

3.3.2000

In Mozambique
terrible floods. A baby
was born in a tree.

We don't know
we're living. We're not
living, perhaps, dry.

From now on
trees will scream at me
when it rains.

Myles Campbell

An Daolag Shìonach

Ann an ceàrn àraidh de Shìona,
san iar-dheas, chan fhada bho bheanntan Iunnàn,
tha seòrsa ùbhlan rim faighinn
a tha cho anabarrach taitneach
's gum biodh na h-ìompairean o shean a' cosg
an òir rin ceannach, is gan tairgse
aig fèisdean 's cuirmeannan san àros mhòr.
Ach cha robh dìreach blas nan ubhal aca.
Leugh mi gu robh daolag coireach ri sin,
nach fhaighear ach air craobhan na ceàirn ud,
's a dh'fhàgas uighean airson tràth a chinntinn
an cridhe nan ubhal. Chan fhan iad ann
gu fad', ach thèid cùbhraidheachd iongantach
a sgaoileadh feadh gach meas. An dèidh don chnuimh
a sgiathan a shìneadh a-mach is teicheadh,
chan fhàgar lorg de fantainn ann ach sgleò
òmarach an lì an ubhail, 's boladh
mìorbhaileach a dh'fhairtlich e
air sgoilearan is gàirnealairean
na cùirt gu lèir a mhìneachadh.

'S e sin a nì mi leis a' chànain seo.

Crìsdean Whyte

The Chinese Beetle

In a particular part of China,
in the south-west, not far from the mountains of Yunnan,
a species of apple can be found
which is so extraordinarily delightful
that the emperors of old used to spend
their gold to buy them, and offer them
at feasts and banquets in the palace.
But they did not really have the taste of apples.
I read that a beetle was responsible for that,
which is found only on the trees of that district
and which leaves eggs for incubation
in the heart of the apple. They do not remain there
long, but a remarkable fragrance
is spread throughout every fruit. When the worm
has stretched its wings and fled,
no trace is left there of its sojourn but an amber
sheen in the apple's hue, and a marvellous
scent that defeated the attempts
of the scholars and gardeners
of the entire court to explain it.

That's what I do with this language.

Christopher Whyte
translated by Ronald Black with assistance from the author

In My Country

walking by the waters
down where an honest river
shakes hands with the sea,
a woman passed round me
in a slow watchful circle,
as if I were a superstition;

or the worst dregs of her imagination,
so when she finally spoke
her words spliced into bars
of an old wheel. A segment of air.
Where do you come from?
"Here," I said, "Here. These parts."

Jackie Kay

Craig MacKay

Myles Campbell

Voyager

Da Nort Boat

Riding northwards, astride the deep,
perspective tilts to meet the horizon.
It is a clear, sharp line; a defining
clarity repossessed.

Whin I come awa, every ness an taing
stabs herd. Da Bard Head, Helliness,
Mousa, Sumburgh. Rowled
i da Roost's lichtless waves
I bide up for Fair Isle ta pass
afore mi sicht-lines geng skave.

taing – low promentary
da Roost – tide race (between Sumburgh Head and Fair Isle);
geng – go
skave – squint

Christine De Luca

Exile

The evening star hung motherpolished bright an inch off the moon's 1950s face. You raised liquid jewels all night in a Canadian bar, then sailed your foreign boat homewards through varying salt breezes.

Lewis floated towards you, smaller, perhaps, than anticipated. You poured an hour's silver tears on the Lewis Public floor, tore the wall off its hinges and ran to the pier where your people's bones first turned to salt.

You clasped two bloodied hands together like a single stiff spearhead and aimed it at the gloomering, pinned-up sky.

You wanted to pray but could remember neither the words themselves nor the accent which fixed them.

You leaped off the pier and, tossing your head back, made a mental note that you had never seen the stars shimmering so bright, so remarkably close. The sea drank you in, its splash tingling all over your body, as tantalising as a kiss.

Kevin MacNeil

Slave

A boat, departing slowly over black water
The town, shrinking
I, nothing.

Suhayl Saadi

Sea-Faring

The global consciousness that arose from the activities of the sailing men meant that the ocean was never regarded as an obstacle to togetherness, but rather as the means to connect one place with another. The coming of everyday air travel in the latter part of this century has meant that the sea is now regarded differently – though perhaps the learning brought home by the merchant seamen has been replaced, and improved upon, by the new technologies. The moment of enlightenment described by astronauts, when they are able for the first time to look back at our planet and see the beautiful blue ball as a whole for the first time, is not so far removed from the knowledge of those who have circumnavigated the world in their ships.

* * *

Beyond the flat earth of the boundaries of sense, he knows –
    The world is just a great round ball folk circle to work and live.
    A global awareness.
    If you spit in the ocean, that drop might reach the nearest shore.
But hoist a sail, and you go where you please, to new found land.

Sie-Færin

Ayont da flat ært
o da boondries o sens,
he kens –

da wirld's choost
a roond bloo baa fok sirkil
t'wirk an liv.

A gloabil awaarnis.
Du spits ida oshin
an a drap myght rekk Æshnis.

Bit hoiest du a sæl
du gjings quhar du will
tæ njoo fun laand.

Robert Alan Jamieson

Constant Star

In the land of 'summer dim', night is a brief darkening, even as dawn is shining above the northern horizon. In winter, darkness invades and tyrannises the day. The lighthouse at Eshaness was a constant in these changing skies, bright summer and dark winter alike, both signalling and receiving: the lamp, a beacon, twinkling; while the keeper's eye scanned the sea, like the 'Gødman' – local term for the 'Good Shepherd'. Now unmanned, the function is only that of star, signalling. The lighthouse no longer sees.

* * *

Summer's dim came down about the cliffs, and up above the crouching body of Eshaness, light lay over the northland like a lacework shawl.

One solitary eye keeps blinking, just as it does in the black heart of winter. All around swells up and dwindles

grows up green and withers away. Moonrise and sunset, neap tide and spring tide.

Constellations drop below the land and others rise to cut a new shape in the changing heavens.

But Eshaness light's always blinking – blink, blink, blinking – a star eye watching, watching and shining.

He thinks – It's good to know the Shepherd's there.

Konstint Starn

Simmerdim kam doon aboot da Niep
an up abøn da krug o Æshnis,
lyght læ owir da nortlaand læk a hap.

Æ solitrie ie's ay blinkrin,
choost is it dös ida blak hert o wintir.
Aa aroond swalls up an dwyns,

grows up grien, dan widders awa –
mønrys an sunfaa,
niep tyd an voar tyd.

Konstelæsjin's drap ablo da laand
an iddirs rys t'kut a njoo shæp
ida chænchin hievins,

bit Æshnis lyght's ay blinkrin –
blink, blink, blinkrin – a starn ie
waatchin, waatchin an shynin.

He tinks – Hit's gød t'ken
da gødman's dær.

Robert Alan Jamieson

Bottled

Hay's of Aberdeen, makers and purveyors of soft drinks, were famed throughout the north of Scotland. Their sweet cordial concentrates, drunk neat despite the 'dilute to taste' instruction, were regarded as a winter treat, given to children in spirit glasses with sweet biscuits when they went out 'guizing' round the houses at the festivals of Halloween, Christmas Eve, Hogmanay and Up-Helly-Aa. The 'message in the bottle' of this poem did find a beachcomber's hand elsewhere, but rather than the foreign shores of Iceland, Norway, Faroe or Denmark, it reached no further than the 'northland' on the other side of St Magnus Bay.

* * *

It was a Hay's ginger cordial bottle he threw beyond the incoming wave, with his handwriting on the paper inside.

Hay's corks twisted tighter, would keep his inky message dry for the world to read.

From this shore, he might reach out to Rekjavik or Tromsø, to Heligoland or Torshavn.

He never doubted a stranger's hand would pick Hay's bottle from an ebbing shoreline somewhere.

Then a letter came. A man had found it in the shallows and wrote with photos from that foreign land across the sea –

Eshaness.

Bottilt

Hit wis a Hæie's chinchir koardjil
he baalt owir da fæs o da wæjiev
wi his haandskrivin 'po da pæpir insyd.

Da Hæie's korks snødit tyghtir,
wid kiep his ingkie messiech
dry fir da wirld t'fin.

Fæ dis laandfaa, he might rekk
oot ta Riekjaviek or Tromsø,
t'Heligolaand or Tor's Havn.

He nivir dootit an ungkin haand
wid lift Hæie's bottil
fæ an ebbin grund sumwy.

Dan dir kam a lettir bakk. A man hed fun it
ida shoormil an he ret wi fotoos
fæ dat ungkin laand akross da sie –

Æshnis.

Robert Alan Jamieson

na h-eilthirich is am BBC

shiud i
a' chailleach
àiteigin air a' Chladach a Tuath
air a glacadh mar ghiomach
anns an uisge
le muinntir a' BhBC

"dh'fhalbh iad," ars ise,
"an fheadhainn òga;
's cha tig duine a chèilidh oirnn
tuilleadh."

dualchas siùbhlach
cràdh an dealachaidh
am fianais sholas
is *mics*
is luchd-amhairc
ri dìdearachd thar a' chuain
a' cur sgleò nan linn
air aithris sliochd nan eilthireach

a' filmeadh sa bhaile iasgaich
far nach fhaigh thu tuilleadh iasg
ach bùth bheag
a reiceas rudeigin car coltach ris
clèibh ghiomach bheaga
mar chuimhneachan air an sgrìob

's an t-seann tè fhathast
an deas-meadhan na sràide
crogain *coke* ma cois
ann an tobar na cuimhne
a' caoineadh an t-sìl
a dh'fhalbh leis an uisge

"cut" "nì sin an gnothach"

Iain S. Mac a' Phearsain

the emigrants and the BBC

there she is
the old lady
someplace on the North Shore
caught like a lobster
in the rain
by the folk from the BBC

"they've gone," she says,
"the young ones;
and no one comes to visit us
anymore."

a migrating heritage
the pain of separation
in view of lights
and mics
and spectators
peeping over seas
lowering the veil of ages
on the recitation of emigrant stock

filming in the fishing village
devoid of any fish
but a small shop
selling something like it
tiny lobster pots
souvenirs of the trip

and the old one still
in the middle of the street
coke cans at her feet
in memory's well
mourning the seed
that left with the rain

"cut" "that'll do"

John S. MacPherson

Thuirt Thu Gun Lasadh Ceud Uinneag

Thuirt thu gun lasadh ceud uinneag
ceud bliadhna air ais na do bhaile
far nach eil a-nochd ach tè do mhàthar
a' deàrrsadh thar na mòintich briste.

Aithnichidh mi an aon aognaidheachd
fa chomhair na fàsalachd annam fhìn
gun aiteal a-nist bhuats'
ag innse dhomh gu bheil thu ann
ged a chroch mi an lampa an àirde
is tha solas a' dòrtadh mun stairsnich.

Meg Bateman

You Said A Hundred Windows Shone

You said a hundred windows shone
a hundred years back in your township
where tonight only your mother's
sends its light over the broken moor.

I know that same desolation
in the emptiness in myself,
with no glimmer from you now
to tell me where you are
though I have hung up the lamp
and light floods the doorstep.

Meg Bateman

Recurrences

That spilt coffee returns and returns,

not in a director's cut –
cast, global, tangible –

but specific – the cup's jump just –
and continually receding.

Receding from touch,
returning and returning to mind.

I think I've learnt my lesson
but the flashbacks don't agree.

Rob MacKenzie

Elsie Mitchell

Meg Bateman
Drawing by Meg's son Colm

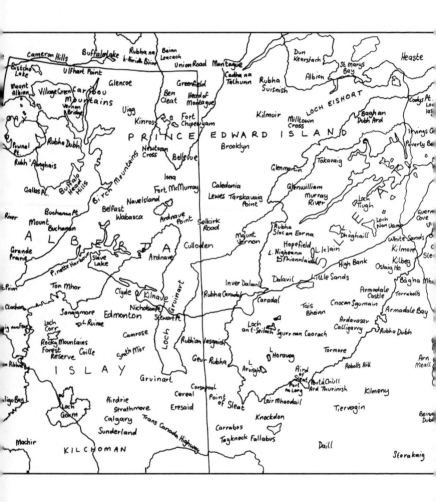

Iain Mac a' Phearsain

Murdo 'Stal' MacDonald

Siùsaidh NicNèill

Scent of Memory

Scent of Memory

I remember the disappointment
of turning a perfect stone to
the side, strewn with moss and dirt.

Dampness lived in the hollow
where stories are told, so
quietly to themselves, we miss them.

A myth by nature is true.
Beetles' trajectory as they scatter
away like the darts of memory.

The pebble is replaced.
Its underside stinks of salt and weed:
print of gathered past.

Shampa Ray

Hinges

On the airstrip: fog.
Nothing taking off.
Five in the afternoon,
more or less.

I'd have called it a 'flitting'
but it was a year before I was born –
to my father it was 'moving house.'
He was Ma's envoy in Scotland:
he'd just chosen a field
that would grow into a bungalow
and he'd pay for it
whenever the bathroom,
opening on the hall
with a frosted glass door,
trapped her, towelnaked,
before the postman
and something to be signed for.

Through the same melted glass
I saw my first memory:
my eldest brother, nine or ten,
was stretching and not touching anything,
petrolburns on his face and hands,
a human X at the front door
(on a building site a friend
had clicked him alight;
we still don't know the bet).

On the airstrip: fog, night.
Eleven o'clock.
My father is being practical
on the hotel phone:
"I am speaking
back in my room."

In the morning in England,
like a new couple
two police officers stood back
as Ma opened the door.
They had to be reassured:
she gave them tea in the fine bone.
(Just beyond the wicker of radar
the first plane out, just past midnight,
had dropped like a figurine.)

In the afternoon
my mother met my father in Arrivals.
Before they held held held each other
he says they just shook hands.

Richard Price

Black and White

Sheila's wedding, the title
of the 1960s cine film.

There she is in her white wedding-dress
on a grey church lawn in Liverpool.
A bunch of white flowers,
a white toothy smile,
and all the white relatives
in their shades of white hats.
Now the white confetti,
the rice, and there he is,
flickering in the background;

a dark Indian shadow
with a walk-on part.

Irfan Merchant

British Perfect

In Ceylon, when a foreman
had words with the Sinhalese
they crushed him under slabs.
All the French were bastards,
Tamils worked the hardest:
there were no troubles then.
        Every Hogmanay
the dam-man received
a levee up-country –
a jeep-day through loud trees
overflowing with stories,
long finished letters for …

Troubleshooting:
the tower
though British perfect
("fast for Jamaicans"), lacked
a quake foundation.
        When the work died
a hurricane keened through.
Planes secured by tractors
still took off:
five unscheduled stops
destroyed Departures.

Leave was postponed.

His reputation built,
my father came home.

Richard Price

Île an Dèidh Cill' Nèimh

a-mach às a' chladh
nam dheann ruith dhan fòn

àgh is cràdh ar daoine
a' cur tachais nam bhroinn

mi fhìn 's cuimhne na cuideachd ud
nar bruaillean air chùl na cuibhle

grèim air a' bhodach
mu dheireadh a-muigh air a' phrèiridh

naidheachd àite-breith athair a sheanar
air a lìbhrigeadh dha mar ìobairt an eòlais

's cha chluinn mi ach guth fann thar a' chuain
"how's the car running?"

Iain S. Mac a' Phearsain

Islay After Kilnave

out of the graveyard
tearing down to the phone

our people's joy and misery
itching me within

myself and memories of them
losing it behind the wheel

a hold of the old fellow
finally out on the prairie

news of his grandfather's father's birthplace
delivered up like the sacrifice of knowledge

and I hear an indistinct transatlantic voice alone
"how's the car running?"

John S. MacPherson

Ealghol: Dà Shealladh

Choimhead mi an t-seann chairt-phuist,
na taighean mar fhàs às an talamh,
na h-aonaichean nam baidealan os an cionn,
nan comharra air mòrachd Dhè,
mus d' rinneadh goireas de bheanntan,
no sgaradh eadar obair is fois,
eadar an naomh is an saoghalta …
is shìn mi chun a' bhodaich i.

"Eil sin cur cianalas ort, a Lachaidh?"
  dh'fhaighnich mi, 's e na thosd ga sgrùdadh.
"Hoigh, òinseach, chan eil idir!
  'S e cuimhne gun aithne a bh' agam oirrese,"
  is stiùir e ri bò air thùs an deilbh.
"Siud a' Leadaidh Bhuidhe, an dàrna laogh aig a' Leadaidh Ruadh –
  dh'aithnichinn, fhios agad, bò sam bith
  a bhuineadh dhan àite seo rim bheò-sa."

Meg Bateman

Elgol: Two Views

I looked at the old post-card,
the houses like a growth from the soil,
the peaks towering above them,
a sign of the majesty of God,
before an amenity was made of mountains,
or a divide between work and play,
between the sacred and the secular ...
and I passed the picture to the old man.

"Does it make you sad, Lachie?" I asked
as he scrutinised it in silence.
"Sad? Bah! Not at all!
I couldn't place her for a moment,"
and he pointed to a cow in the foreground.
"That's the Yellow Lady, the Red Lady's second calf –
I'd know any cow, you see,
that belonged here in my life-time."

Meg Bateman

from Dissolving Song

III
How in the beginning it was winter.
Now spring sails over the Waitemata
on my last day in the country of my childhood
(Is it that country?)

This evening we'll head over to Manurewa
to my father's cousin just home from Europe
(from Don's family in Lewis (lost and found)
from Leslie in London, my father in Yorkshire)
she gives me a photograph to take back
of the two of them on Ashness bridge (See that's Jean
Eileen and George Sweet's daughter   And that's Al
Charlie's eldest, who married Geraldine Macfarlane)
Twenty years since we last did this:
a tradition I tell her

But before then I will already have packed my clothes
the rolls of colour film   my notebook
(the books gone last week   two boxes, surface)
I will have packed the earrings the apple the bowl

the spoons the found shells   I will have packed
the wave-eaten ring in which a gastropod
once encoded its miraculous spiral
and it will sing there in my luggage
as it will sing in the hold of the 747
as it lifts with me into the southern hemisphere midnight
as it sings to me now

spiralling between something and nothing
simply found   meaningful

Gerrie Fellows

Nature Poems

This is my spring poem

For the clock-forward coffee
jolting me into more alert grumpiness
For the dandruff puff of flea powder
on my cat's one hundred new friends
For people smiling in offices –
damn them all to hell –
And for the first cuckoo in our street
to get his lawn mower out

This is my summer poem

For the bubble gum and chlorine
of children outside the pool
For my Factor 20 legs
fun-sliding on the hot car seat
For the rubbery bather
stretching after its long hibernation
For my dog-biscuit heels
exfoliating on warm tarmac

This is my autumn poem

For the fragrant sari
of a sheet fresh from the dryer
For the red, gold, green-for-go
through the trickling filter of a wet windscreen
For the kebab of birds
that waits on the line for the scones that went wrong
For the back-to-school shavings
of twelve coloured pencils

This is my winter poem

For the crusty baked towel
on the immersion heater
For the jigsawed corners catching
on the carpet pile
For technicolour musicals
on dark afternoons
And the nylon lightning
of a cold midnight strip

Siân Preece

For Starters

Love
Indian, Chinese
And Italian too.

Race is
Not an issue
With me

So long as
The service
And food

Are good.

Hamid Shami

David Williams

Robert Alan Jamieson

Bhangra!

Bhangra

BHANGRA!
At college
At counter
At nothing in particular
Come to the Bhangra!
Reds and yellows
Blues and greens
A psychotic rainbow
Painted in Hell
And brought to earth
On the back
Of the Beast
Dancing colours
Wild, hot music
Sitars and synthesizers
Twitching shoulders
Girls in clusters
Like firecrackers
Boys in gangs
Ten or twenty
Leering and sneering
No sweat, man
Cool
Comments passing
Heardunheard
Lewd as Hell
Then the music
And the dancing

Electrical Punjabis
Loud as Hell
Boys with boys
Girls with girls
In circles
Rings
Of light and sound
Electrical Punjabis
Round and round.

Suhayl Saadi

National Colours

I
The teams picked and lined-up in rank,
we jogged onto the school football pitch
like iambs on a sonnet's green rectangle,
limbering-up for the big metre.
There we were, high with the fresh
juice of adolescence in our shorts –
the keen ones, jittering like wound-up
clockwork toys, in Scotland strips;
my kit was from *What Every Woman Wants*.

The rhythm of the game settled itself
as the ball was passed along the wing
in an *a-b-a-b* rhyming scheme.
Then: "*Up the Pairk!*" bellows Mr Phillips
the P.E. teacher, and so a boy belters the ball,
soaring, opening up the field: "*On Yersel
Big Man!*" But it's intercepted by the defence,
as the sestet turns the game around,
finishing with a nifty headered couplet.

Always the odd one out, I was busy
watching the steam spout from my lips
as I walked slowly between the goals,
a caesura through the classical mould. Then:
"Eerie-Fanny Get Yer Arse In Gear!"
(Or it was *Earwig, Irvine, Fanny-Face*; or
Paki-Bastard, Shoe-Shine Boy, Get Back Home:
the mysterious dervish name from Persia
whirled on the thick-set tongue of Ayrshire).

Minded of Ghandi's epic salt march
I kept on my measured pace
quietly disrupting the maths of the game;
and by the final whistle,
my boots were as muddy as the rest.

II

At home, football was just not cricket;
my dad wanted me to bat for India
or England, depending who was beating Pakistan.
"When in Rome, do as the Romans do"
was his mantra, and as the history master
at St Peter's European Boys School,
Panchgani, taught him by rote
the Kings and Queens of England
and the civil order of innings and over,

we were the Romans in a Pictish town.
So at Cambusdoon Cricket Club
I polished spin bowling weekly,
mastering the wily Oriental 'googly'.
And my dad has a photo of me framed
in a V-neck pullover and long white trousers
with green and orange stains;
feet clasped, knees just bent
and a bat posed forever at my toes:

I peer out from a pudding-bowl fringe
as if still batting at the crease;
waiting for the next bowl
like an Indian boy
who knows his place.

Irfan Merchant

Do' Care

In a Paris hotel lounge on one occasion
My thirteen year old five foot five
Daughter glowed with the attention
Of three young men striving
To pigeon-hole her Scottishness
And break her brittle brusqueness
With their far-eastern finesse.

If Scotland played England
Whom would she support
– Sco'land – was the answer delivered
And if England played India
– India – she claimed with a triumphant swagger
If England played Germany
– Germany – was the response
From the unassailable position
Of a new-found nationalism.

And what if it were Scotland and India
One demanded with the diabolical confidence
Of an argument-winning lawyer –
She clamped down her glass, shrugged her bare
Shoulders, turned away saying – do' care.

Bashabi Fraser

Cash 'n' Carry

Seven-hundred-and-twenty moons and five children later,
Gross turnover three million pounds and five pence,
Maker of bonbons, maker of candies,
Deals under the carpet,
Deals over the carpet,
Itherutherhitherthither
Altogether
Dead.

Suhayl Saadi

Young Chinese and Scottish

These bastards I feed.
I serve them sourfaced
from this lair's fiery kitchen,
dish up oodles of rich-crispy-chicken
in an atmosphere thick
with soy, sweat and steam.

Ape-drunk, certain, they'll swagger in,
pie-eyed and slobbering on my thin
silken blouse: "(Hur hur) Hello rare
mah wee China doll, er …
Ah'll havvuh speshl (hur hur) sixty-nine
(hur hur) uhna bedduh speshl flied lice."

My folks tell tales of dragons, but I have tasted haggis!
See, Buddha-sure, I just hunger for dancing, drinks
and a Scot I adore. How I love to not
taste homesweethome in his plain Scottish food.
I'll serve no more. Take away
the Chinese till I'm half understood.

Kevin MacNeil

I'm a Racist

'If this is a paki, a darkie and a chinky, you're a racist.'
  – *slogan on a poster produced by the City of Edinburgh Council, with three appropriate head-and-shoulder photos.*

I saw a paki
on the side of a bus.

I'm a paki.

I thought to myself:

How nice. A paki
on the side of a bus.

Irfan Merchant

On the Street

I wear myself like an old coat
With pockets full of empty bottles
Jingling as I run
Trying to catch up with something or other.

I move myself along
And nod to short sleeved policemen
Who are young, almost boyish
Grinning through their teeth
Folding their bare arms
To talk to strangers.

With Freddy Clark I leave the office
A business lunch with clients
Who know how much they're worth.
We drink and laugh to impress the waitress
And ogle her to impress each other.
We talk awhile about a file
And point and burp and laugh out loud.

Back at the office phones are ringing
But no one is there to listen.

We saunter back in alcohol
Breathing jokey fumes.
We're businessmen in grey and blue
Wearing our suits like jewellery.
Cutting you a glance short and sharp
With our serious minds, our serious moves
Walking in our serious shoes
And standing straight
And, always, well outside of us, is you.

Gerry Singh

bho A' Mheanbhchuileag

Innsidh mi seo dhut –
chan e Atlas a th' annam;
chan urrainn dhomh an saoghal a ghiùlain.
Chan eil annam ach atam air druim an domhain,
ri strì eadar fisean is fiùisean.

Tha e a' cur dragh orm
a' faicinn dùthaich a' dol fodha
mar chaisteal-gainmhich fon làn,
is cànain air tilgeil uainn
mar bhratach phàipeir ghlas,
's *weltanschauung* air dearmad
mar aisling-latha fhaoin,
is eachdraidh air dol à fianais
mar lorg-coise cloinne air an tràigh.

Innsidh mi seo dhut –
chan e Fionn a th' annam;
chan urrainn dhomh mo dhùthaich a ghiùlain.
Chan eil annam ach cealla am bodhaig Albainn,
ri strì a bhith nam chealla-eanchainn.

Tha mi beag 's tha eagal orm roimh rudan beaga:
a' chealla aillseach a sgriosas bodhaig,
am facal òinseach a sgriosas gaol,
am bonn-airgid a reiceas rìoghachd,
an t-atam sgoilt a sgriosas Hioroisimea,
a' vìoras nimheil, am peilear nàimhdeil,
mearachd ann an inntinn feallsanaich.

Dh'ionnsaich mi rud –
tha mi bàsmhor;
is dòcha gun tig a-màireach às m' aonais.

Bu toil leam a bhith mar Mhaois,
a' sgrìobhadh bhriathran Dhè;
ach bhriseadh clàr-cloiche am peann plastaig agam.
Agus a bharrachd air sin
chan eil preas loisgeach agamsa
mar choinneil.

Fearghas MacFhionnlaigh

from The Midge

I'll tell you this –
I'm not Atlas;
I cannot bear the world.
I am only an atom on the surface of the globe,
struggling between fission and fusion.

It troubles me too
to see a country sink
like a sand-castle beneath the tide,
and a language thrown from us
like a faded paper flag,
and a *weltanschauung* forgotten
like an empty daydream,
and history disappear without a trace
like a child's footprint on the beach.

I'll tell you this –
I'm not Fionn;
I cannot bear my country.
I am only a cell in Scotland's body,
struggling to be a brain-cell.

I am small and fear small things:
the cancer cell that destroys a body,
the stupid word that destroys love,
the coin that sells a kingdom,
the split atom that destroys Hiroshima,
the poisonous virus, the enemy bullet,
a mistake in the mind of a philosopher.

I learned something –
I am mortal;
maybe tomorrow will come without me.

I would like to be like Moses,
inscribing the words of God;
but a stone tablet would break my plastic pen.
And besides
I have no burning bush
for a candle.

Fearghas MacFhionnlaigh

Pride

When I looked up, the black man was there,
staring into my face,
as if he had always been there,
as if he and I went a long way back.
He looked into the dark pool of my eyes
as the train slid out of Euston.
For a long time this went on
the stranger and I looking at each other,
a look that was like something being given
from one to the other.

My whole childhood, I'm quite sure,
passed before him, the worst things
I've ever done, the biggest lies I've ever told.
And he was a little boy on a red dust road.
He stared into the dark depth of me,
and then he spoke:
"Ibo," he said. "Ibo, definitely."
Our train rushed through the dark.
"You are an Ibo!" he said, thumping the table.
My coffee jumped and spilled.
Several sleeping people woke.
The night train boasted and whistled
through the English countryside,
past unwritten stops in the blackness.

"That nose is an Ibo nose.
 Those teeth are Ibo teeth," the stranger said,
 his voice getting louder and louder.
 I had no doubt, from the way he said it,
 that Ibo noses are the best noses in the world,
 that Ibo teeth are perfect pearls.
 People were walking down the trembling aisle
 to come and look
 as the night rain babbled against the window.
 There was a moment when
 my whole face changed into a map,
 and the stranger on the train
 located even the name
 of my village in Nigeria
 in the lower part of my jaw.

 I told him what I'd heard was my father's name.
 Okafor. He told me what it meant,
 something stunning,
 something so apt and astonishing.
 Tell me, I asked the black man on the train
 who was himself transforming,
 at roughly the same speed as the train,
 and could have been
 at any stop, my brother, my father as a young man,
 or any member of my large clan,
 Tell me about the Ibos.

His face had a look
I've seen on a MacLachlan, a MacDonnell, a MacLeod,
the most startling thing, pride,
a quality of being certain.
Now that I know you are an Ibo, we will eat.
He produced a spicy meat patty,
ripping it in two.
Tell me about the Ibos.
"The Ibos are small in stature
not tall like the Yoruba or Hausa.
The Ibos are clever, reliable,
dependable, faithful, true.
The Ibos should be running Nigeria.
There would be none of this corruption."

And what, I asked, are the Ibos' faults?
I smiled my newly acquired Ibo smile,
flashed my gleaming Ibo teeth.
The train grabbed at a bend,
"Faults? No faults. Not a single one."

"If you went back," he said brightening,
"the whole village would come out for you.
Massive celebrations. Definitely.
Definitely," he opened his arms wide.
"The eldest grandchild – fantastic welcome.
If the grandparents are alive."

I saw myself arriving
the hot dust, the red road,
the trees heavy with other fruits,
the bright things, the flowers.
I saw myself watching
the old people dance towards me
dressed up for me in happy prints.
And I found my feet.
I started to dance.
I danced a dance I never knew I knew.
Words and sounds fell out of my mouth like seeds.
I astonished myself.
My grandmother was like me exactly, only darker.

When I looked up, the black man had gone.
Only my own face startled me in the dark train window.

Jackie Kay

Catriona Grant

Richard Price

168

Siân Preece

And My Fate Was Scotland

And My Fate Was Scotland

Fate brought me to Scotland. I found it cold, its colours softer than I was used to, the birds quiet. In Khartoum, the sun had made everything sharp and smelly. The sun bleached the colours of the washing hanging out in the yard. A special blouse or new shirt had to be hung up to dry in the shade. We spent a lot of time looking for shade.

The view from Sudan is that the entire West is one place; tearless, affluent and all-powerful. In the Blue Nile Cinema I watched American films and British films and couldn't tell them apart. The people looked the same, spoke the same language and behaved in the same 'Western' way, that is they knew better than their parents and rushed around dropping things. After a diet of Hollywood, Scotland was shockingly cloudy, all that grey a mistake.

If I could not tell Britain and America apart in the cinema, I could scarcely tell Scotland and England apart when I arrived. The train from London went on and on, on and on – yes, it would have been quicker to take the Eurostar to Paris. Paris, France, out of the UK. The passengers of the Flying Scotsman were very patient. They ate sweeties and crisps, more sweeties and crisps and the Firth of Forth came and stayed in my memory, the water not blue like the Nile. When the train arrived in Aberdeen, the air was more wonderful than London's summer, fresher. But it was only the different Bank Holidays that convinced me that I was living in another country. To me people in Scotland and England looked the same; they spoke the same language and behaved in the same 'British' way, that is saying please, sorry and thank you all the time.

My alarm at my first Mums and Toddlers meeting - a mother holding up a biscuit out of reach of her son. 'Say please first'. And then after the poor child stuttered and struggled and succeeded in getting hold of the biscuit, it was 'Say thank you' before he was allowed to gobble it up. All the mothers I had known in Sudan (including myself) were too eager to get as much food inside their children as possible to give any regard to politeness. They coaxed and bullied, waiting for the little mouth to open so they could pop in just one more spoonful. Greetings instead were all important when I was a child in Khartoum. A child had to greet an adult, shake hands, stand up if an adult came into a room. Because I was a girl, I had, in addition to the handshake, to kiss all the aunties whether they were family or not. I got extra points if I smiled and remembered their names. Even among children, greetings were important. If I forgot to say hello to a friend in Secondary school (and that included a kiss as well), she would say with sarcasm, 'Did I sleep last night at your house?'

I moved to Scotland and had to learn new ways in order to get on in life or even just cope. In order not to become superfluous, which could easily happen. The European in Africa is entitled to be there. The African in Europe is *de trop*. He comes and stands back because that is what is expected. Because everything (the locals believe) has already been sorted out and organised, there is nothing really new that he can add. But if we don't add something, we are not living. Put couscous in the English dictionary, Ramadan, pray in a place where people have stopped praying. If we don't add something or change something then why did Fate bring us here?

Gradually I learned to distinguish between the English and Scottish accents. I was able to tell immediately if a sitcom was American or British. It was easy to pick up that it was 'Yes, please' and 'No, thank you', in that way, that order. And don't ask a lot of questions; find out things for yourself. Follow maps, read signs, look up things in the Yellow Pages. This was a reading culture not a speaking one. My shock coming from Sudan where the vast majority could not read and write, to where everything was written down. Everything. I picked up a bottle of shampoo and read: 'DIRECTIONS: Lather and rinse thoroughly. Repeat if required. In case of contact with eyes, rinse with water immediately.' I asked myself, 'Were there people in Britain who did not know how to use shampoo?'

Sometimes I asked people for directions and they didn't reply, just pointed towards a sign. I learned that I was expected to search for signs and read them before asking. (A child growing up in Britain would know this simple fact, but for the outsider it has to be learned.) The sheer abundance of leaflets. How to wean your baby, how to cope with a bereavement, how to clean your wok …. It became a household chore to get rid of unwanted words. In Khartoum, old newspapers were used to wrap sandwiches for school. Buy a book, fresh bread or a leg of lamb and you would get it wrapped up in yesterday's copy of *The Days*. When I was in the University of Khartoum, the student newspaper was hand-written and hung up on a board. As soon as the latest issue came out there would be a rush and everyone would crowd round to read it. We would stand on tiptoe to read the top pages, sit on our heels to read the bottom. Tissue paper was so expensive and such a luxury that I remember sitting in the library with a toilet roll on my desk because I had a bad cold. There were no leaflets in the library.

Yesterday, I saw a man walking in Great Western Road carrying a baby in his arms without a sling, without a pushchair. I was surprised and wondered if there was some sort of emergency. Yet, in Sudan, babies were carried in their father's or mother's arms all the time. That was their mode of transport, no pushchairs and no slings. Pushchairs and slings were not manufactured locally. The only ones available were imported from abroad and a Sudanese baby in a pushchair was a baby born with a silver spoon. After years in Scotland, I knew that every Scottish baby had a pushchair whether it was brand new, second or third-hand. My eyes had become used to all the signs of Western affluence; dogs in the back seats of cars and furniture in good condition left out on a skip. That man carrying a baby in his arms, without a pushchair or a sling, looked unusual, a memory from a faraway place.

When I first came to Scotland I used to wonder why everyone became so happy and rushed outdoors as soon as the sun started shining. I couldn't understand why they went about saying, 'What a lovely sunny day!' It was just normal for me, and still too cool. The sun shining – that was what the sun was supposed to do, that was what the sun had done every single day in Khartoum. I couldn't understand why they said, 'Lovely day'. I thought, 'A normal day, finally, after months of rain'. Now years later I began to feel as happy as everyone else and agreed, 'It's a lovely day'. I began to take rain and grey clouds for granted and not sunshine anymore.

I moved from heat to cold, from the Third World to the First – I adjusted, got used to the change over time. But in coming to Scotland, I also moved from a religious Muslim culture to a secular one and that move was the most disturbing of all, the trauma that no amount of time could cure, an eternal culture shock. I left a way of life connected to the source. I moved from a place where death was close and pervading like Scotland's clouds, where sadness was a friend. A life different from the West's. The language was different. 'I will see you next week, if Allah wills it to be', 'You did so well in your exam *al-hamdulillah* - thanks to Allah', 'This is very sad news, may Allah compensate you', 'Thank you for your help, may Allah reward you'. Years in Scotland and I still cringe when someone says, 'I'll definitely be there'. How do they know? How can they be sure? It's smoother to my ears to hear, 'I'll be there *insha' Allah*: I'll be there, God willing'.

I found in Scotland very little knowledge of Islam or the Sudan, the two things that made up my identity. What people knew was as accurate as the view I'd had of Britain watching 'Carry On' films at the Blue Nile

Cinema. I hid my homesickness. It was my big secret, not to be acknowledged, not to be expressed. I was twenty-seven, twenty-eight, twenty-nine and I had a lovely family but I had to push myself through every day. Back and forth, I went to the GP with various pains and infections. I ate antibiotics. Did I experience racism? I was too busy grieving to be sure.

One day I went to an aromatherapist. She asked me questions and filled up the answers in a sheet. 'Any mood swings? Psychological problems?' 'I'm homesick,' I said for the first time and laughed because I was embarrassed. She put her pen down and looked at me. And because she looked at me, straight at me, she became my first friend. 'That's terrible,' she said, 'I got it when I went to college. Homesickness is living in the past.' She gave me a bottle of Clary Sage to take home. I'm not sure if the Clary Sage, worked but her words made a big impression on me. Homesickness was living in the past. I did not want to live in the past, I was too young to live in the past.

I searched for an insight, a rationale. Why did Fate bring me to Scotland? Why did Fate take me away from my home? It was a breakthrough when I found an answer. In the pages of a paperback entitled *Winter Lectures*, simple words written for me.

Everything coming against our desires is only coming by our Lord's will. If we know this we can attain peace and surrender. When we stop fighting, then His will may lead us easily to our destination without trouble or fatigue. Prophets and saints are like this; they reached Paradise in this life. Sometimes I say al-hamdullilah *my will is not happening. His will is best.*

Leila Aboulela

Chila Kumari Burman

Hamid Shami

Author and Photographer Notes

Author Notes

Leila Aboulela

Leila Aboulela was born in Cairo in 1964 and brought up in Khartoum, Sudan. She moved to Britain when she was in her mid-twenties, and now lives in Aberdeen. She writes mostly in prose, and her first novel, *The Translator*, (Polygon) was long listed for the Orange Prize 2000.

Meg Bateman

Meg Bateman was born in Edinburgh in 1959 to English parents. She learnt Gaelic in South Uist and at Aberdeen University. She now teaches at Sabhal Mòr Ostaig, the Gaelic college on Skye. Themes of human relationships and family life recur in her work, but, above all, she is a poet of romantic love. Her most recent collection of poems *Aotromachd agus Dàin Eile/Lightness and Other Poems* was published by Polygon in 1997.

Maoilios M.Caimbeul, Myles Campbell

Myles Campbell was born in Staffin on the Isle of Skye in 1944, where his father was a lay preacher of the Free Church. This Gaelic-speaking Calvinist environment had a profound effect on his sense of identity and much of his work deals with the tensions between the religious and rationalist outlook. His most recent collection, *A' Gabhail Ris* was published in 1994 by Gairm. He is currently working on a novel. He lives in Skye, a few miles from his childhood home, and teaches Gaelic in Wester Ross.

Gerrie Fellows

Gerrie Fellows was born in New Zealand in 1954. Her family moved to London when she was a child. She has lived in Glasgow since the age of 30, where she works as a writing tutor. She is also a keen mountaineer. Her most recent collection is *The Powerlines* was published by Polygon in 2000.

Bashabi Fraser

Bashabi Fraser was born in West Bengal, India in 1954. As a child she moved from Calcutta to London, and then to Darjeeling. She attended a British school in India, where she was taught in English. Bashabi first came to Edinburgh in 1985, has lived here since 1994 and is an Associate Lecturer at the Open University and a Post-doctoral Fellow of the Centre for South Asian Studies at

Edinburgh University. She is also an expert in North Indian classical dance. *Life* was published by Diehard in 1997 and in 1996 she co-edited *Peoples of Edinburgh, our multicultural city* (with Helen Clark and Lorraine Dick, published by City of Edinburgh, Department of Recreation, Museums & Galleries). She is currently editing the letters between Patrick Geddes and Rabindranath Tagore, to be published by Visva-bharati.

Rody Gorman

Rody Gorman was born in Dublin in 1960. He writes poetry in Irish, Scottish Gaelic and English. He moved to Skye in 1987 where he works at Sabhal Mòr Ostaig. His most recent book is *Cùis-Ghaoil,* published by Diehard in 1999.

Robert Alan Jamieson

Robert Alan Jamieson was born in Shetland on Up-Helly-Aa 1958, where he grew up in the crofting communities of Sandness, speaking 'Sjetlin' or Shetlandic. He is currently writer in residence at the Universities of Glasgow and Strathclyde. His most recent publication is the 'skewed fairytale', 'Crossing a Mountain', in *Mount Hiddenabyss*, a collaboration with the painter Graeme Todd (Fruitmarket Gallery, Edinburgh 2000). The three poems published here are from a book-length sequence of 27 poems, plain translations and notes, entitled 'Nort Atlantik Drift'.

Jackie Kay

Jackie Kay was born in Edinburgh in 1961 and now lives in Manchester with her son. In the past she has acknowledged the influence of her black, Scottish and female identity on her work. Her three published collections of poems include *The Adoption Papers*, which tells the story of a black girl's adoption by a white Scottish couple, and her most recent, *Off Colour*, published by Bloodaxe in 1998. Her first novel, *Trumpet* (Picador, 1998) won The Guardian Fiction Prize.

Christine Laennec

Christine Laennec was born in San Francisco in 1960. She moved to Scotland in 1992 and currently teaches in the Departments of French and Women's Studies at the University of Aberdeen where she is studying Gaelic. Her poetry has appeared in various magazines, and she is currently working on a first novel, based in the north-east.

Christine De Luca

Christine De Luca was born in Shetland in 1947. She moved to Edinburgh to study, and works there as an educationalist. De Luca writes in both English and Shetlandic. Her most recent collection *Wast wi da Valkyries* was published by The Shetland Library in 1997, and was awarded the Shetland Literary Prize.

Iain S. Mac a' Phearsain, John S. MacPherson

John S. MacPherson was born in Edmonton, Canada in 1965. Growing up in a Gaelic community he came to Scotland in 1996. He writes in Gaelic, French and English and is clear that his commitment to Gaelic implies internationalist sympathy for all minority languages. His poetry has appeared in *New Writing Scotland* and recent pocketbooks. He lectures at Sabhal Mòr Ostaig.

Murdo 'Stal' MacDonald

Murdo 'Stal' MacDonald was born in Stornoway, Lewis in 1969. He grew up in Upper Coll, a crofting community, with Gaelic as his native tongue. He writes his poetry in this language, drawing on the "bottomless well" of Gaelic culture.

Fearghas MacFhionnlaigh

Fearghas MacFhionnlaigh was born in the Vale of Leven, Dunbartonshire in 1948. He was brought up in Canada and Scotland and is now an art teacher in Inverness. A Gaelic learner, his last collection *Bogha-frois san Oidhche/ Rainbow in the Night,* was published by the Handsel Press in 1997.

Rob MacKenzie

Rob MacKenzie was born in Glasgow in 1964. He was brought up in Glasgow and on the Isle of Lewis, where he learnt a smattering of Gaelic, which is reflected in the frequent combination of Gaelic and English in his work. His largest collection, *Off Ardglas*, was published by Invisible Books in 1997. He currently lectures at Lancaster University.

aonghas 'dubh' macneacail

aonghas macneacail was born in Uig on the Isle of Skye in 1942 and grew up in a community which was then entirely Gaelic speaking. He is currently writer in residence at Brownsbank Cotage, near Biggar. He writes in both English and Gaelic, and his most recent collection of poems, *Oideachadh Ceart/A Proper Schooling*, published by Polygon in 1996, won the Saltire Prize.

Kevin MacNeil/ Caoimhin MacNeill

Kevin MacNeil was born on the Isle of Lewis and currently lives on Skye. He writes in Gaelic and English and is the inaugural Iain Crichton Smith Writing Fellow for the Highland Council. His first collection of poems, *Love and Zen in the Outer Hebrides*, was published by Canongate in 1998. He is the first person from this country to win the Tivoli Europa Giovani International Poetry Prize. His work has been translated into 10 languages.

Irfan Merchant

Irfan Merchant was born in Liverpool in 1973 of Indian descent. From the age of three months he was brought up in Ayr and now lives in Edinburgh. His poems have appeared in various magazines and in *The Redbeck Anthology of British South Asian Poetry* (Redbeck, 2000).

babs nicgriogair

babs nicgriogair was born on the Isle of Lewis in the summer of love and is a native Gaelic speaker. She describes herself as a peace activist and 'langscape artist', and has in the past 'waited on tables, turned tables, pulled pints and pushed Penguins'. She works with writing, visual arts and theatre.

Siùsaidh NicNèill

Siùsaidh NicNèill was born in 1955 and raised on the Isle of Lewis where she learned Gaelic. Her work has been anthologized, and her collection of poems, *All My Braided Colours*, was published by Scottish Cultural Press in 1996. She has travelled widely and now lives on Skye working in a Gaelic nursery.

Siân Preece

Siân Preece was born in Neath, South Wales. She moved to Scotland in 1994 after living in Canada and France . She lives in Aberdeen. Her first book, a collection of short stories, *From the Life*, was published by Polygon in 2000.

Richard Price

Richard Price was born in Reading, England, in 1965, but moved to Renfrewshire at the age of six weeks. Since 1988, he has lived in London. He is Curator of Modern British Collections at the British Library, and a founding editor of *Southfields* magazine. His most recent collection, *Perfume and Petrol Fumes*, was published by Diehard in 1999. He is co-founder of Vennel Press.

Shampa Ray

Shampa Ray was born in 1967 in India and brought up in Scotland. She speaks Bengali and English. She has published in *Fox*, *Wellspring*, *Spectrum* and *ALP* publications. Shampa currently lives in Kirkcudbrightshire.

Suhayl Saadi

Suhayl Saadi was born in Yorkshire in 1961, six years after his parents arrived from Pakistan. He was brought up in Glasgow where he now lives and works as a doctor. His poems and short stories have appeared in various magazines as well as *Macallan Shorts 1999* published by Polygon.

Hamid Shami

Hamid Shami was born in Pakistan in 1969 and brought up in Glasgow. He is a frequent contributor to *Scotland's Oracle*, an independent multicultural newspaper. These poems belong to an early period of his writing, which, as Hamid acknowledges, was driven by anger, and which he feels he has recently moved away from.

Gerry Singh

Gerry Singh was born in Glasgow in 1957. He describes his family background as unknown, his Scottish identity as "deeply hidden within", and his Indian roots as "painted on my face". The poems included in this collection reflect a period of work directly concerned with these issues of identity and dislocation, while more recent work shows a growing interest in landscape. He is now a teacher in Perthshire. His poetry is featured in *The Redbeck Anthology of British South Asian Poetry*.

Christopher Whyte

Christopher Whyte was born in Glasgow in 1952. A Gaelic learner, his work as poet, editor and critic has shown a determination that the Gaelic tradition should reflect contemporary life. His anthology of contemporary Gaelic poets, *An Aghaidh na Siorraidheachd/In the Face of Eternity* was an important contribution to the Gaelic Renaissance. He lives in Edinburgh and teaches in the Department of Scottish Literature at Glasgow University. His collection *Uirsgeul/Myth* was published by Gairm in 1991 and his fourth novel *The Cloud Machinery* will be published in October 2000.

Photographer Notes

Chila Kumari Burman

Chila Kumari Burman was born in Liverpool of Indian descent. Her work has been recently exhibited in *Jewel in the Crown* (Berlin and Hamburg NGBK) and *A Grand Design* (Victoria and Albert Museum).

Catriona Grant

Catriona Grant was born in Dunfermline in 1964. She was part of *The Art of Documentary* exhibition at the Scottish National Portrait Gallery, and is currently studying for an MSc in Electronic Imaging at Duncan of Jordanstone College of Art and Design.

Craig Mackay

Craig Mackay was born in Inverness in 1960 and considers himself an indigenous Highlander. His work was exhibited in *A Portrait of Ghosts* at Art.tm, Inverness in April 2000.

Elsie Mitchell

Elsie Mitchell was born in Coatbridge, Scotland in 1966. She was part of the *Mac Totem* exhibition that toured the Highlands and Islands in 1998. She currently works as the Visual Arts Education Officer at An Lanntair, the arts centre in Stornoway.

Iseult Timmermans

Iseult Timmermans was born in 1969 of English and Dutch descent, and her immediate family includes Indian, Turkish and Scottish siblings. Most recently, she has been selected as one of eleven artists commissioned to produce work for *No Small Feat*, due to be exhibited at Street Level in March 2001. She is currently co ordinating a series of projects with children and young people for Street Level Gallery, Glasgow.

David Williams

David Williams was born Edinburgh in 1952. His work has been most recently exhibited in *Stillness and Occurrence* at the Zelda Cheatle Gallery in London, September 2000.

Index of Authors

Aboulela, Leila 27, 42, 177–81
Bateman, Meg 56–57, 104–105, *109*, 126–27
Caimbeul, Maoilios M. / Campbell, Myles 74–75, *82*
De Luca, Christine 55, 91, *173*
Fellows, Gerrie 28–29, *47*, 128–29
Fraser, Bashabi 72–73, *136*, 150
Gorman, Rody 38–39, *87*
Jamieson, Robert Alan 94–99, *139*
Kay, Jackie 78, 160–63, *166*
Laennec, Christine 69
Mac a' Phearsain, Iain S. / MacPherson, John S. 60–61, 100–03, *111*, 124–125,
MacDonald, Murdo 'Stal' 70–71, *113*
MacFionnlaigh, Fearghas *85*, 156–159
MacKenzie, Rob *51*, 62–63, 106
macneacail, aonghas 64–65, *141*
MacNeill, Caoimhin / MacNeil, Kevin 15–20, 92, 152, *185*
Merchant, Irfan 30, 122, *135*, 146–49, 153
nicgriogair, babs 32–35, 40–41, *49*
NicNèill, Siùsaidh 68, *115*
Preece, Siân 130–31, *171*
Price, Richard 120–21, 123, *169*
Ray, Shampa 119
Saadi, Suhayl 93, 144–45, 151, *187*
Shami, Hamid 23, 31, 58–59, 66–67, 132, *189*
Singh, Gerry 36–37, *45*, 154–55
Whyte, Crìsdean / Whyte, Christopher 76–77, *81*

Acknowledgements

Thanks are due to the following copyright holders for permission to reproduce the poems in this collection. While every effort has been made to trace and credit copyright holders, the Publishers will be glad to rectify any oversights in any future editions.

MEG BATEMAN: 'Ealghol: Dà Shealladh/ Elgol: Two Views' from *etruscan reader ix,* by Fred Beabe, Nicholas Moore & Meg Bateman, (© etruscan books 2000); RONALD BLACK: 'The Chinese Beetle' (English translation) from *An Tuil,* edited by Ronald Black (published by Polygon, 1999; translation reprinted by permission of Ronald Black); GERRIE FELLOWS: 'Dissolving Song III' from *The Powerlines* (© Polygon, 2000); JACKIE KAY: 'In my country' from *Other Lovers* (© Bloodaxe, 1993) and 'Pride' from *Off Colour* (© Bloodaxe, 1998); AONGHAS MACNEACAIL: 'an tùr caillte/ the lost tower' from *A Proper Schooling and other poems/ Oideachadh Ceart agus dàin eile* (© Polygon, 1996); KEVIN MACNEIL: 'Exile' and 'Young Chinese and Scottish' from *Love and Zen in the Outer Hebrides* (© Canongate, 1998).

Thanks also to the following anthologies and magazines where the following work is published:

LEILA ABOULELA: 'And My Fate Was Scotland', *Deliberately Thirsty* 6, 2000; ROB MACKENZIE: 'Lewis Punk Bands of the early 1980s', *Off Ardglas* (Invisible Books, 1997); FEARGHAS MACFHIONNLAIGH: Extract from 'A' Mheanbhchuileag/The Midge', *An Tuil* (Polygon, 1999); IRFAN MERCHANT: 'I'm a racist', *The Redbeck Anthology of British South Asian Poetry* (Redbeck, 2000); BABS NICGRIOGAR: 'An Gàidheal/The Pakistani' and 'An Duine Dubh/The Highlander', *Edinburgh Review* Spring 1998; HAMID SHAMI: 'Lost', *New Impact Journal* Feb/Mar 1997, 'My Talented Cousin', *Other Poetry* 1998; GERRY SINGH: 'India Gate', *The Redbeck Anthology of British South Asian Poetry* (Redbeck, 2000) and 'On the Street', *Cutting Teeth,* 1999.

pocketbooks

Summer 1998

01 GREEN WATERS
    An anthology of boats and voyages, edited by Alec Finlay;
    featuring poetry, prose and visual art by Ian Stephen,
    Ian Hamilton Finlay, Graham Rich.
    ISBN 0 9527669 2 2; paperback, 96pp, colour illustrations, reprinting.

Spring 2000

02 ATOMS OF DELIGHT
    An anthology of Scottish haiku and short poems, edited with an
    Introduction by Alec Finlay, and a Foreword by Kenneth White.
    ISBN 0 7486 6275 8; paperback, 208pp, £7.99.

03 LOVE FOR LOVE
    An anthology of love poems, edited by John Burnside and
    Alec Finlay, with an Introduction by John Burnside.
    ISBN 0 7486 6276 6; paperback, 200pp, £7.99.

04 WITHOUT DAY
    An anthology of proposals for a new Scottish Parliament, edited
    by Alec Finlay, with an Introduction by David Hopkins. *Without
    Day* includes an Aeolus CD by William Furlong.
    ISBN 0 7486 6277 4; paperback with CD, 184pp, £7.99 (including VAT).

Autumn 2000

05   WISH I WAS HERE
An anthology representing the diversity of cultures, languages and dialects in contemporary Scotland, edited by Kevin MacNeil and Alec Finlay, with an Aeolus CD.
ISBN 0 7486 62812 paperback, 208pp, £7.99

06   WILD LIFE
Walks in the Cairngorms. Recording fourteen seven-day walks made by Hamish Fulton between 1985 and 1999, *Wild Life* includes an interview with the artist by Gavin Morrison and an Aeolus CD.
ISBN 0 7486 62820 paperback, 208pp, £7.99

07   GRIP
A new collection of darkly humorous drawings by David Shrigley, *Grip* is the largest collection of Shrigley's work published to date and includes 16 colour illustrations and an Afterword by Patricia Ellis.
ISBN 0 7486 62389 paperback, 208pp, £7.99

Spring 2001

08   DISTANCE AND PROXIMITY
      The first collection of Scottish poet Thomas A. Clark's prose
      poems, *Distance & Proximity* includes the ever-popular *In Praise of
      Walking*, as well as a number of previously unpublished works,
      accompanied by the suggestive textures of Olwen Shone's
      photographs.
      ISBN 0 7486 6288X paperback, 208pp, £7.99

09   THE WAY TO COLD MOUNTAIN
      A Scottish mountains anthology weaving together poetry, nature
      writing and mountaineering adventures, edited by Alec Finlay,
      with photos by David Paterson.
      ISBN 0 7486 62898 paperback, 208pp, £7.99

10   in memory of the scottish forests
      A litany of the names of the lost Caledonian pine forests gathered
      by Dutch artist herman de vries; also including a species list
      compiled by de vries and Scottish Natural Heritage, and an
      interview with the artist by Paul Nesbitt.
      ISBN 0 7486 62901 paperback, 208pp, £7.99

Available through all good bookshops.

Book trade orders to:
Scottish Book Source, 137 Dundee Street, Edinburgh EH11 1BG.

Copies are also available from:
Morning Star Publications, Canongate Venture (5), New Street,
Edinburgh EH8 8BH.

Website: www.pbks.co.uk

Wish I Was Here

An Aeolus CD by Leila Aboulela, Suhayl Saadi and babs nicgriogair

1. Leila Aboulela   5 mins
   recorded Aberdeen, April 2000

2. Suhayl Saadi   5 mins
   recorded Glasgow, May 2000

3. babs nicgriogair   5 mins
   recorded Glasgow, May 2000

Running time 15 mins

Recorded out in the 'real world', not a recording studio, these are voices
embedded in the acoustic environment that they inhabit. Listening to
these voices, to what they say and the specific texture and substance of
the words, we hear the desire to speak evoked in the speaking. This
audio work aims to create a sense of place, the place of the recording
and the place that is the individual voice and experience.

Zoë Irvine, May 2000

Recorded and designed by Zoë Irvine.
Produced and mastered at Aeolus.

© Leila Aboulela, Suhayl Saadi and babs nicgriogair
© Aeolus 2000

Email: aeolus_sound@yahoo.com
phone: (44) 7775 540 969